Cheetah
Accelerated
EXAM PREP WORKBOOK

Workbook
The Cheetah Success Series

Cheetah Accelerated EXAM PREP WORKBOOK

The Fastest Way to Pass Your Test

Michelle LaBrosse, PMP

MAKLAF PRESS
Carson City, NV

Cheetah Accelerated Exam Prep Workbook
by Michelle LaBrosse, PMP
Published by MAKLAF Press LLC.
502 N. Division St., Carson City, NV 89703
A Division of MAKLAF Holding, Inc.
www.cheetahlearning.com

Copyright © 2007 by MAKLAF Press LLC. All rights reserved. Printed in the United States of America. Except as permitted under the United States Copyright Act of 1976, no part of this publication may be reproduced or distributed in any form or by any means, or stored in a database or retrieval system, without the prior written permission of the publisher.

Notice: This publication contains the opinions and ideas of the author. It is intended to provide helpful and informative material on the subject matters covered. It is not meant to replace the advice of an attorney. The author and publisher specifically disclaim any responsibility for any liability, loss, or risk, personal or otherwise, which is incurred as a consequence, directly or indirectly, of the use and/or application of any of the contents of this book.

Post-It®, Sharpie® and all other brand, product, service, and company names are trademarks of their respective holders. Reference to a product, service, or company does not imply recommendation, approval, affiliation, or sponsorship of that product, service, or company by either the authors or MAKLAF Press.

Cover and interior design by Pneuma Books, LLC. Visit www.pneumabooks.com

ISBN 13: 978-0-9761749-7-4

Printed in the United States of America

12 11 10 09 08 07   6 5 4 3 2 1

*To all of the Cheetah Learning students
who have successfully used our techniques
to pass the PMP exam.*

Contents

Introduction to the Accelerated Exam Prep Workbook 1

Part 1 : Peak Performing Mind 5
   Tips for Improving Mental Performance 5
   Peak Performing Mind Action Plan 7
   What Will the Plan Do for You? 8
   Activity 1 : Peak Performing Mind Project Feasibility Study 8
   Analyze Your Results 8
   Activity 2 : Develop Your Peak Performing Mind Action Plan 8
   Activity 3 : Peak Performing Mind Menu 8
   Activity 4 : Peak Performing Mind Shopping List 8
   Shopping Tips 9
   Table 1 : Example Lifestyle Changes for Peak Performing Condition 10
   Table 2 : Your Lifestyle Changes for Peak Performing Condition 11
   Table 3 : Example Peak Performing Mind Action Plan 12
   Table 4 : Your Peak Performing Mind Action Plan 13
   Table 5 : Daily Peak Perfoming Mind Menu 14
   Table 6 : Peak Performing Shopping List 15

Part 2 : Rapid Synthesis and Instant Recall 17
   Color Coding 17
   Timing 18
   Creating Mind Maps 18
   Figure 1 : Mind Map Card Example 19
   Activity 5 : Rapid Synthesis Organization Worksheet 20
   Table 7 : Example of Rapid Synthesis Organization Worksheet 20
   Table 8 : Your Rapid Synthesis Organization Worksheet 21
   Cheetah Sheets 22
   Figure 2 : Sample Cheetah Sheet 22
   Instant Recall Tips 23

Part 3 : Relaxed Focused Concentration... 25
    Breathing Exercises 25
    Figure 3 : Breathing Exercises Worksheet................................. 26
    Yoga Stretches 26
    Table 9 : Yoga Stretching Examples... 27
    Baroque Music 27
    Psychoacoustic CDs 28

Part 4 : Structured Study Time.. 31
    Structured Study Time Plan Outline 31
    Activity 6 : Structured Study Plan 32
    Figure 4 : Structured Study Plan Roadmap.............................. 32
    Table 10 : Pre-study Preparation 33
    Table 11 : Example Daily Study Schedule................................. 34
    Table 12 : Your Daily Study Schedule 35

Part 5 : Conclusion and References 37

"The accelerated immersion approach for preparing for the Project Management Professional certification exam was the greatest learning method I've ever used. I now use the mind mapping and flash techniques on every test for which I have to prepare... I learned how to learn. I have already recommended this course to three colleagues."
— Ron Hunt, PMP, Project Manager

Accelerated Exam Prep Workbook

An Integrated Approach to Reduce Study Time and Improve Performance

Once you learn the power of the techniques presented in this program, you'll most likely be just like Ron — you'll use them forever. I've used a variety of the techniques presented in this workbook throughout my life. For example, I received a Bachelors of Science in Aerospace Engineering with honors, even though in high school I scored 35% on an aptitude test for engineering. I was able to graduate at the top of my class in engineering because I used many of the techniques presented in this workbook. I still use many of these same techniques today in my professional development.

Throughout any career, we are faced with situations that are tests — whether actual exams, or just very stressful situations that test our metal. In this workbook, you'll develop an action plan to significantly reduce the time you spend preparing for exams, and at the same time, you'll significantly improve your performance on your tests.

These techniques work for students of any age, and they work well. We use this process to help prepare people to pass a very difficult exam for project management certification. In one year, we captured more than 20% of the market of people who purchase programs to prepare for this exam. Word of mouth caused our sales to spread like wildfire. Many of our students asked us to put together a generic program that they could use with their children, as well as on other exam preparation applications. This workbook is the result of that request.

The Accelerated Exam Prep processes in this workbook provide a variety of techniques integrated at different stages of exam preparation in order to speed up exam preparation and to improve overall performance on an exam. We have tested this process extensively with tens of thousands of people since our first group in September 2001. Most people spend about 180 hours or more in preparation for this exam. Our students spend less than 50 hours.

Success leaves clues, and here is the trail. This method has worked for thousands of others, and it can work for you, too. You will achieve the levels of success of which you know you are capable.

    Michelle LaBrosse, PMP
    Chief Cheetah
    Cheetah Learning®
    The Fastest Way to Reach Your Goals

THE METHOD

The method involves:

- **Peak Performing Mind** — Adopting diet, exercise, and lifestyle habits that aid in mental performance.

- **Rapid Synthesis** — Using rapid synthesis techniques to quickly assimilate a large amount of content in a way that speeds instant recall.

- **Relaxed Focus** — Integrating music, yoga, breathing exercises, and psycho-acoustic technology to put your mind into a state of relaxed concentration and to improve your test-taking confidence.

- **Structured Study Time** — Visual planning tools to map out an easy-to-implement exam preparation plan.

I designed this document as a workbook so that you can use it to structure your own program.

"Old habits are strong and jealous."
– Dorothea Brande

Peak Performing Mind

Achieving Peak Mental Performance through Diet, Exercise, and Lifestyle

What you eat and how you take care of your body significantly impact your ability to quickly prepare for an exam. They also impact your performance on the actual exam. There are a number of ways you can put your body and mind in peak performing states so you can significantly reduce the time you need to study, while at the same time dramatically improving your performance on exams.

At the end of this section, we provide:
- Activities that will help you get your mind into peak performance.
- Suggested menu plans.
- A menu-planning template.
- A shopping-list form so you can be prepared with the supplements and food you'll need while you're studying.

CAUTION

As with any of the advice presented here, be sure to check with your doctor to evaluate how various recommended diet, exercise, and lifestyle habits will impact you. Every person is different, but these tips have been found to work for the vast majority of people. If you are under the care of a doctor for ANY medical condition, be sure to clear it with him or her prior to embarking on any of the recommended tips.

TIPS FOR IMPROVING MENTAL PERFORMANCE

I want to share with you what we've learned by studying the effects of diet, exercise, smoking, and sleep on mental performance — the type of mental performance you'll need to do well on your exam. Many of the tips reproduced here can be found in numerous other publications. If you would like more information, we recommend *Boost Your Brain Power* by Ellen Michaud and Russell Wild, editors of *Prevention* magazine.

1. **Vitamins** are key — specifically B-complex vitamins, C, and E. We recommend that you get 500 mg of C, 400 mg of E, and a general B-complex vitamin. Check out http://www.realage.com for more information about the importance of vitamins in achieving peak mental performance. Make sure that you check with your doctor about the vitamin supplements that are right for you.

2. **Caffeine** — Studies have shown that while caffeine can get your mental gears moving, it can actually cause you to make more errors if you have to solve complex mathematical problems. If you have a very strong coffee habit, consider reducing your dependency on caffeine a month or two before the test.

3. **Alcohol** — A number of studies have shown that alcohol kills brain cells that impact memory-recall ability. You may want to abstain from alcohol up to a month (or at least a week) before starting the preparation for your exam to ensure your brain is in peak condition.

4. **Protein vs. Carbohydrates** — It has been shown that protein stimulates an amino acid called tyrosine. Tyrosine boosts mental performance so strongly that it has been shown to overcome the mind-muddling effects of stress. To achieve the best benefits, we recommend you either abstain from eating carbohydrates, such as bread and fruit, or eat them about 10 minutes after you've had the protein. On the morning of your test, eat a high-protein breakfast and limit or eliminate the carbohydrates. (This means eat the eggs, and forget the toast, cereals, and pancakes.) You can take breaks during the exam to eat snacks; we recommend you bring a couple of the protein-type bars that are on the market today. Eat a large breakfast so that you won't get hungry for several hours afterwards. Definitely do not have coffee and donuts for breakfast the morning of the test or while you are studying. Consult your doctor if you're concerned about how this dietary change will affect you.

5. **Exercise** — Studies have shown that people who exercise routinely think better, remember more, and react more quickly than those who don't exercise at all. Working up a sweat by walking, jogging, or swimming for 20 minutes at least three times a week is best for your brain. If you haven't exercised in a while, check with your doctor before starting an exercise program. Also, exercise is a proven stress release. We recommend you start on an exercise program at least a month before taking the exam. During your exam prep time, take a break about every 90 minutes to do a short series of yoga stretches and a simple, yet effective, breathing exercise. You'll learn how to do this breathing exercise in the section on Relaxed Focus. Every day you are studying we also recommend that you take a relaxing walk, or do your full workout routine.

6. **Prescription & non-prescription drugs**
Check with your doctor about any prescription drugs you are taking if you're concerned about their effects on your mental performance. It goes without saying that if you are into "recreational" (illegal) drugs, you should abstain while you are preparing for the exam. The short-term memory loss effect of marijuana is well documented. If the FDA has neither approved it for memory improvement, nor sanctioned the lab manufacturing it, you have no idea what it is that you are actually ingesting.

7. **Other memory-enhancing supplements**
There have been numerous studies done on the memory-enhancing effects of gingko biloba. While we are not recommending you take this supplement to prepare for your exam, if you feel that it helps you, then it probably does. However, check with your doctor. Gingko biloba interacts with prescription medicines and may cause adverse reactions in some people.

8. **Cigarette smoking** — You guessed it — better if you don't. Non-smokers were found to have higher recall rates than smokers. If you smoke and are thinking of quitting, do so well before you take the exam. It will affect your memory even more if you're going through nicotine withdrawal. If you've already quit smoking, don't start again. While you might think it could help calm your test-taking nerves, it will instead impact your test-taking performance. If you're a committed smoker, just realize you may have to put more effort into recall than non-smoking test-takers.

9. **Sleep** — Get an adequate night's sleep at least every night for a week before you start studying and especially right before the exam. If you have infants or young children at home, or if you live in an environment where your sleep is often interrupted, we recommend you stay in a comfortable, quiet hotel several nights before your exam. (To make certain that it's quiet, find out if there are large groups with late-running parties also staying at the hotel, or if there is late-night construction work happening outside the hotel.) For our program, we found that people who stay at a hotel perform better on the exam; so even if you live in the area, consider staying at a hotel. If you're taking the exam a distance from your home, it's better to stay in a hotel near the exam location than to get up early to drive there. Refrain from drinking alcohol the night before the exam. Limit your caffeine consumption (as mentioned previously), get adequate exercise, and eat more carbohydrates later in the day so you can get restful sleep. You can create your own relaxation CD at www.bwgen.com to put you into a deep sleep. You also can create a daytime exam prep CD to listen to (see page 28.)

PEAK PERFORMING MIND ACTION PLAN
Why an Action Plan?

The intense pursuit of high performance on an exam, especially exams that are gateways to your future success in your professional endeavors, is equivalent to running a marathon. In very short periods of time, you can learn and assimilate material to a level of comprehension that takes most people up to five times longer to accomplish. To do this, your mind has to be in peak condition. The activities you'll do as part of the peak performing mind project will improve your chances of success on your exam.

What Will the Plan Do for You?

To significantly reduce your test preparation time and increase your exam performance, your mind must be in peak condition. How your mind performs is directly related to how well you take care of your body. With these activities, you'll develop and implement a project plan to put your mind in peak performing condition.

ACTIVITY 1 — PEAK PERFORMING MIND PROJECT FEASIBILITY STUDY

Table 1 on page 10 is a sample Peak Performing Mind Project Feasibility Study that shows lifestyle changes for peak performing condition.

Using Table 1 as an example, fill out Table 2 on page 11 to indicate how many lifestyle changes you'll have to make in order to put your mind in peak performing condition, and how feasible it will be that you'll be able to achieve several changes to improve your mental performance. (Estimated time to complete — 1 hour.)

Analyze Your Results

The higher the number, the more feasible it is that you can make changes that will significantly improve your mental performance. For achieving a peak performing mind, even trying helps. For example, if you currently drink four cups of coffee, it is better for your mental performance if you can cut back to just one. It's always feasible to attempt to improve your health — the question is, are you motivated to do so? This feasibility study shows you how far you have to go.

ACTIVITY 2 — DEVELOP YOUR PEAK PERFORMING MIND ACTION PLAN

Table 3 on page 12 is a sample Peak Performing Mind Action Plan.

You can get your mind in peak-performing condition both during your exam prep time and during your exam. However, it does take some planning. Also, if you make sure you have your basic survival needs met once or twice per week, you can better focus on preparing for the exam.

Using Table 3 on page 12 as an example, fill out Table 4 on page 13 for your Peak Performing Mind Action Plan. Use the menu plans and shopping list. You can make copies of the menu plans and shopping list; make a new one every week, per your action plan. (Estimated time to complete — 1 hour.)

ACTIVITY 3 — PEAK PERFORMING MIND MENU

Table 5 on page 14 is your Peak Performing Mind Menu. Circle your options and then determine what you already have and what you need to purchase. The key to studying effectively is to eliminate the caffeine, cut way back on the carbohydrates, protein-load while you are studying and on the morning of the exam, and drink plenty of water. If you are studying for more than a week, use these tables and menu suggestions for each week.

ACTIVITY 4 — PEAK PERFORMING MIND SHOPPING LIST

Table 6 on page 15 is your Peak Performing Mind Shopping list and includes recommendations. Use this table to create your own list from the recommendations and bring the list to the grocery store with you on shopping day.

Shopping Tips

Below are a few shopping tips to help you select the right foods for your peak performing mind menu:

1. Stay on the perimeter of the grocery store. This is where the healthier foods are.

2. You are not dieting this week. Fuel your body and don't let yourself get hungry.

3. Stay away from overly processed foods and those with a high sugar content.

4. Do not purchase chocolate or anything with caffeine in it.

5. Do not purchase sports drinks. They contain too much sugar and some contain caffeine.

The following pages feature Tables 1 through 6. Use them to complete the preceding activites.

Table 1 **EXAMPLE LIFESTYLE CHANGES FOR PEAK PERFORMING CONDITION**

TIP	Conformance (rate from 1-5)	Time before Start of the class (in days)	Feasibility Index (conformance X time)
Take vitamins B, C, & E	3 (take every so often)	45	135
Give up caffeine	3 (gave up coffee for decaf, still drink diet coke)	45	135
Give up alcohol	3 (cut back)	45	135
Eat more protein in the AM	2 (I'll have to stop the trips to Dunkin Donuts)	45	90
Exercise at least 1/2 hour a day	3 (not as often as I should)	45	135
Limit drug usage	5 (never did, never will)	45	225
Don't smoke cigarettes	5 (never did, never will)	45	225
Get adequate sleep	2 (I have two small children, get real)	45	90
		Total	1170

Table 2 <u>YOUR</u> LIFESTYLE CHANGES FOR PEAK PERFORMING CONDITION

TIP	Conformance (rate from 1-5)	Time before Start of the class (in days)	Feasibility Index (conformance X time)
Take vitamins B, C, & E			
Give up caffeine			
Give up alcohol			
Eat more protein in the AM			
Exercise at least 1/2 hour a day			
Limit drug usage			
Don't smoke cigarettes			
Get adequate sleep			
		Total	

One — Peak Performing Mind

Table 3 EXAMPLE PEAK PERFORMING MIND ACTION PLAN

TASK	TIME	HOW OFTEN	WHEN
Set Goals Examples: 1. Easy to implement 2. Non-intrusive day-to-day 3. Effective — I feel good 4. Speedy — it works fast 5. I can stick with it	30 minutes	Once a week	Sunday evening
Plan menu and put together grocery list	10 minutes	Once a week	Saturday morning
Go shopping	40 minutes	Once a week	Saturday morning
Exercise every day	60 minutes	Daily	When I wake up
Listen to an exam prep daytime CD	30 minutes	Daily	2:00 - 2:30
Listen to an exam prep nighttime CD	30 minutes	Daily	10:00 - 10:30 (at bedtime)
Get adequate restful sleep	7 - 8 hours	Daily	10:00 PM - 6:00 AM

Table 4 **YOUR PEAK PERFORMING MIND ACTION PLAN**

	TASK	TIME	HOW OFTEN	WHEN
	Set Goals Examples: 1. Easy to implement 2. Non-intrusive day-to-day 3. Effective — I feel good 4. Speedy — it works fast 5. I can stick with it			
	Plan menu and put together grocery list			
	Go shopping			
	Exercise every day			
	Listen to an exam prep daytime CD			
	Listen to an exam prep nighttime CD			
	Get adequate restful sleep			

Table 5 **DAILY PEAK PERFORMING MIND MENU**

DAY	BREAKFAST	SNACK	LUNCH	SNACK	DINNER	SNACK	HAVE TO PURCHASE
Sunday	Eggs, breakfast meats, tofu fruit smoothie, milk, yogurt, melon	Cheese, nuts, banana, apple, yogurt with nuts	Chef salad, chicken breast, veggies, steak, fish, soup, fruit	Protein bar, nuts, cheese, beef jerky	Chef salad, chicken breast, veggies, steak, fish, soup, fruit, small amount of pasta	Toast, popcorn, fruit, warm milk	
Monday							
Tuesday							
Wednesday							
Thursday							
Friday							
Saturday							

Table 6 **PEAK PERFORMING MIND SHOPPING LIST**

RECOMMENDATIONS	YOUR LIST
<ul><li>Vitamins —<ul><li>B Complex 1000 mgs</li><li>Vitamin E 400 mgs</li><li>Vitamin C 500 mgs</li></ul></li><li>Two dozen eggs</li><li>Yogurt</li><li>Milk</li><li>Tofu</li><li>Cheese</li><li>Butter</li><li>Bananas</li><li>Strawberries</li><li>Pineapple — canned</li><li>Apples</li><li>Lettuce</li><li>Celery</li><li>Avocados</li><li>Broccoli</li><li>Orange juice</li><li>Beef jerky</li><li>Nuts</li><li>Cheese</li><li>Chicken breasts</li><li>Steak</li><li>Fish</li><li>Soup</li><li>Pasta</li><li>9 protein bars (1 for each day and 2 for exam day)</li><li>Popcorn</li><li>Multigrain bread</li><li>8 AA batteries (for your portable CD or tape player)</li><li>Sugar-free mints (1 pack per day of studying and 2 packs for exam day)</li></ul>	

"Memory is the cabinet of imagination,
the treasury of reason, the registry of conscience,
and the council chamber of thought..."
— Saint Basil

Rapid Synthesis and Instant Recall

Speeding Up Learning and Remembering What You Learn

To speed up your learning and to better remember what you have learned, you need to use several strategies. Mind mapping is a technique you can use to quickly assimilate the material that you need to know for the exam. Mind mapping, combined with various graphical and color recognition strategies, aids in instant recall. These techniques are based on three basic facts that are well known about memory:

1. **People remember in pictures** — The more multi-sensory the image, the stronger your memory will be.

2. **People remember in locations** — If you can place these multi-sensory images in locations on a page, then you'll speed your recall of the information.

3. **People remember in "chunks" of information** — Small bits of images that you place in retrieval areas in your mind help you to better retain information.

To develop your overall rapid synthesis plan for studying the material on your exam, you must become familiar with the following areas.

COLOR CODING

Assign a specific color to each major content area. This will significantly reduce review time later on when you can rapidly go to areas where you need more review and quickly pick those areas out because of their color. Assign the colors of the sections, and ultimately your mind-map cards, in a way that has unique meaning for you. For example, in our Project Management Accelerated Exam Prep course where we use this method, any material associated with budget and cost is color coded green (the color of money). Review your reference resources and assign a color to each large content area. If you are studying an area with nine distinct content areas, select nine unique colors that symbolize the nature of each content area and create 3 x 5 index cards using those colors. In doing this, you'll categorize any material relating to the content by these colors. For example, if you collect a number of references for each content area, catalog it by that color. In this way, you'll speed up being able to locate specific material during your review process.

TIMING

To rapidly synthesize a large amount of material that will be on the exam, try to "mind map" that material. Do this in short, rapid segments on color-coded mind-map index cards. Outline the material you need to study, and assign a short period of time to read and mind map the sections. For example, if you're reading a 10-chapter book, and each chapter has five main sections, set aside no more than 15 minutes to mind map each section. In each section, identify chunks of material that you can summarize on one 3 x 5 mind-map card in approximately three minutes. A little time planning here will significantly speed up your study time. Mind mapping is explained in greater detail further on in this workbook.

Do an initial overall review of the layout of the reference material, and then decide the logical breakdown of the material and how it will fit on your cards. For example, many reference books use numbering conventions such as section 1.0, 1.1, 1.2, subsection 1.2.1, 1.2.2, 1.2.3, 1.2.4, etc. You can make a mind-map card for each sub-section.

Next, determine the relative heading of each card for the section, depending on how the material is organized. This can be very simple. It can be based only on the headings in the reference material you are trying to process. Make all your cards ahead of time, with the heading title on one side.

Then assign the amount of time you'll take to do each mind-map card. Give yourself more time to redo your first several cards. Since you are making the cards before you do the mind mapping, write the assigned time to do the card right on the card. We recommend that you plan on redoing your first three to five cards until you have the process down. Then you'll know what information to put on your cards and how to draw your cards the fastest way possible to quickly process a large amount of information.

Perform your mind-mapping activities for no more than 60 minutes in one sitting. Take a 5- to 10-minute break; get up and walk around, get some water, take a bio break, and do some stretching. If you do this, you'll remember far more than if you sit in a chair for hours mind mapping material that you need to know for the exam.

CREATING MIND MAPS

Mind maps are summary pictures of material that you are studying. Mind mapping is a fast and effective way to summarize and capture key points that you need to remember for your exam. We recommend you make your mind maps on 3 x 5 index cards. This way, you can quickly review them and speed instant recall of key concepts for your exam. If you are a visual

Figure 1 **MIND MAP CARD EXAMPLE**

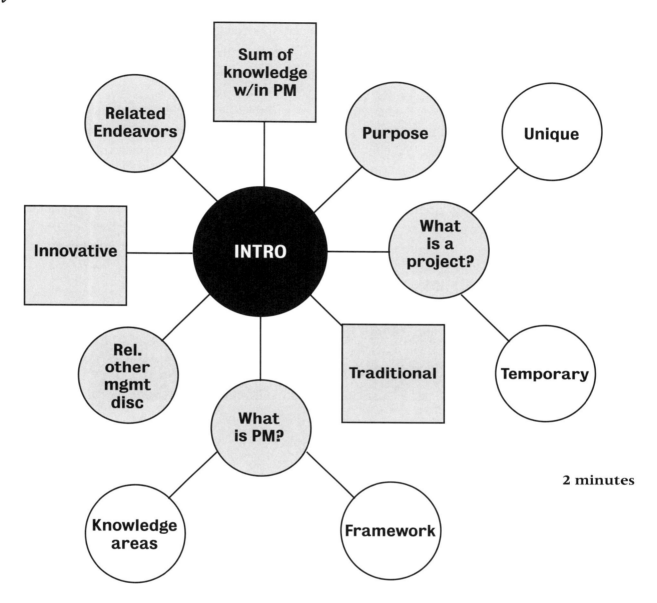

2 minutes

learner, make sure you have a variety of colored markers to organize your mind-map cards. Use a different color for various hierarchical levels of information (for example, title in blue, main points in red, sub-points in green.) Figure 1 illustrates a mind-map card that summarizes the overall chapter of a project management text where we use this methodology. It is a good idea to make the first card of every new chapter a summary card of the entire chapter, because it helps your brain better organize the material in the references.

Figure 1 above shows the amount of time allocated to creating the card and uses gray circles to denote the main sections of the chapters, white to denote the sub-sections, and squares to summarize the overall essence of the chapter. You can choose your own colors.

The picture you make will speed your review time of the content, and the locations and the color of the content will aid in instant recall. The overall organization, and your ability to understand the logical structure of the material you are studying, will significantly speed up synthesis and aid in instant recall of the key points within the material. The timing of the cards helps to maintain focus and concentration. Write the key heading on the front of each card so that once the entire set of cards is complete, you can use the cards as flash cards to quickly review the material you need to know for your exam.

ACTIVITY 5 — RAPID SYNTHESIS ORGANIZATION WORKSHEET

Table 7 below is a sample of the organization of rapid synthesis topics we use to help people study for the Project Management Professional Certification Exam.

Table 8 on page 21 is a blank worksheet provided for you to organize your rapid synthesis efforts. You can pick up color-coded card stock at Kinkos, Staples, Office Max, and many other office supply stores. Make sure to select your colors based on the card stock that the particular store carries. Cut the card stock in four equal segments and use these to make your mind map cards.

Table 7 **EXAMPLE OF RAPID SYNTHESIS ORGANIZATION WORKSHEET**

CONTENT AREA	COLOR	REFERENCE SECTION	NUMBER OF PAGES / CARDS	TIME	WHEN
PM Framework	Lavender	PMBOK® Guide	30 / 15	60 minutes	Monday AM
Integration	Orange	PMBOK® Guide	20 / 10	40 minutes	Monday AM
Scope	Cobalt Blue	PMBOK® Guide	30 / 22	60 minutes	Monday PM
Cost	Green	PMBOK® Guide	30 / 17	60 minutes	Tuesday AM

Table 8 <u>YOUR</u> RAPID SYNTHESIS ORGANIZATION WORKSHEET

CONTENT AREA	COLOR	REFERENCE SECTION	NUMBER OF PAGES / CARDS	TIME	WHEN

CHEETAH SHEETS

In many exams, you are provided scratch paper to work out problems while you are taking the exam. Create a Cheetah Sheet — a fast way to memorize and record all the critical information you need for an exam — that you'll memorize before you go into the exam, which you can reproduce in under 10 minutes at the start of your exam using the scratch paper provided.

After mapping out the content for the exam, identify the key information you need to know for the exam. Create a one-page (8 1/2 x 11) summary sheet with this key information, and memorize it. Create mnemonics that are funny to you, so that you can instantly recall the information on the Cheetah Sheet. By using mnemonics that are humorous, you'll reduce your stress level during the exam and also stimulate instant recall.

There are several things to remember when creating your Cheetah Sheet:

1. Your brain remembers in locations, so make sure you put boxes and other shapes around key information. When you practice reproducing your Cheetah

Figure 2 **SAMPLE CHEETAH SHEET**

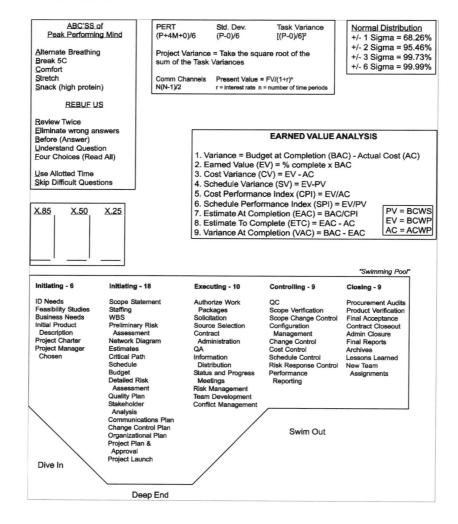

Sheet, keep the same material in the same location every time.

2. Create funny pictures and mnemonics that will help you remember the material on the sheet. You'll need to laugh during the exam if you want to be able to remember things well, so make your sheet funny for you. Don't worry if it isn't funny to anyone else — this is your Cheetah Sheet.

3. Practice, practice, practice! If you stay focused, you can get your Cheetah Sheet down in less than three days by spending less than one half-hour on it every day. Make sure you practice doing your Cheetah Sheet at least twice a day after you have gotten it down.

4. With all this practice you might begin to think that you don't actually need some of the information you originally put on your Cheetah Sheet. However, when you are in the exam, merely having the Cheetah Sheet present will reduce your exam anxiety.

INSTANT RECALL TIPS

The biggest thing you can do to improve your abilities at instant recall is to stay relaxed. Laughing is the number one stress reliever. As stated before, make sure you put things on your Cheetah Sheet that will make you laugh. Also, find opportunities to laugh while you are studying, especially about content areas that you find especially stressful. Make up absurd examples and scenarios about the material that will make you laugh. We make up crazy characters for our students in all our examples and make the test questions very funny and bizarre. We set up the test questions so they are representative of the concepts on the exam, but we make them funny and absurd.

State conditioning is also very good for stimulating instant recall. We have our students eat sugar-free mints while they are creating their mind map cards and Cheetah Sheets, and while they are answering practice exam questions. Then, during the actual exam, we have them eat their mints throughout. This creates a "state conditioning" situation and significantly enhances instant recall for many people. The senses of smell and taste are the strongest memory senses. When they smell a scent again, most people can recall where it was that they first smelled it. For example, if your mother wore a specific perfume when you were a child, you will likely recall childhood experiences you had when you smell that scent.

Most people go through about a roll of mints per day. Depending on where you take the exam, the proctors may not let you take anything into the exam room. If you offer to unroll the mints and let them know you need them to quench a nagging cough that will be disruptive to others in the exam, they will usually let you take them in. If you run into a tough spot during the exam and pop a mint in your mouth, you'll be amazed at the effect it has on your memory.

During the exam, make sure you get up and stretch, take a bio break, and do breathing exercises at least every hour. For those of you who have severe test anxiety, we recommend you stop and do breathing exercises every 10 minutes. These breaks will significantly enhance your instant-recall abilities and will enhance your overall performance on the exam.

"Quiet minds cannot be perplexed or frightened but go on in fortune or misfortune at their own private pace, like a clock during a thunderstorm."
—Robert Louis Stevenson

Relaxed Focused Concentration

Using Relaxation Techniques to Improve Concentration

The mind absorbs new material when it is in a state of relaxed concentration. Mental processing capabilities are dramatically improved in a settled, quiet mind, versus an anxious, stressed mind. This state of relaxed concentration can be acquired by using some very old and some very new techniques. To help people enter into a relaxed and focused mind state, the Accelerated Exam Prep process uses five different agents: alternative-nostril breathing, a series of yoga stretches called the "sun salutation," studying with Baroque music playing (selections with the beat primarily at 60Hz), and two types of psychoacoustic tapes made specifically to put participants into deeply relaxed states while they listen and repeat positive affirmations about their exam-taking capabilities.

BREATHING EXERCISES

Perform a set of 10 alternative nostril-breathing repetitions hourly while you are studying. You should also remember to do these repetitions 90 minutes before any practice or actual exam and each hour during the exam. To perform this technique, hold one side of your nose closed while breathing deeply in through the other side. Before exhaling, switch sides and exhale through the nostril that was just closed. Repeat by inhaling through the same nostril that was closed. Before exhaling, switch sides and exhale through the nostril that was just closed. In yoga, this is called Prayana breathing. It aids in calming your mind, focusing your attention, and reducing anxiety.

Some people claim that it helps in balancing the right and left hemispheres of the brain, but we have not found substantial evidence to validate these claims. Use this breathing technique to calm and focus your mind. Figure 3 provides a worksheet with step-by-step directions and illustrations.

You can use this technique prior to listening to either the daytime or nighttime CD, before doing any practice or real exam, or whenever you need a pick-me-up or to calm down. It is well-proven to relax and rejuvenate.

YOGA STRETCHES

We use a series of yoga stretches that help to calm and center the mind and the body. When people are studying for long periods of time, their bodies tend to be in one sedentary position. Over time, this can cause headaches, backaches, and fatigue. Every 60 to 90 minutes during your accelerated exam prep study period, you'll do what is known as the sun salutation — a series of yoga stretches that can be completed in approximately three to five minutes. You should also do these yoga stretches once every hour during the actual exam. See Table 9 for a worksheet showing how to do these stretches.

YOGA STRETCHING EXAMPLES

Table 9 on page 27 provides instruction and example yoga stretches. You do not need to get into special exercise clothes to do these stretches. You will need to get on the floor for a very short period of time, so if you are in an area with a dirty floor, you may want to put down a towel. The purpose of these exercises is to stretch in order to rejuvenate your body and your mind. Do this series of stretching exercises

Figure 3 **BREATHING EXERCISES WORKSHEET**

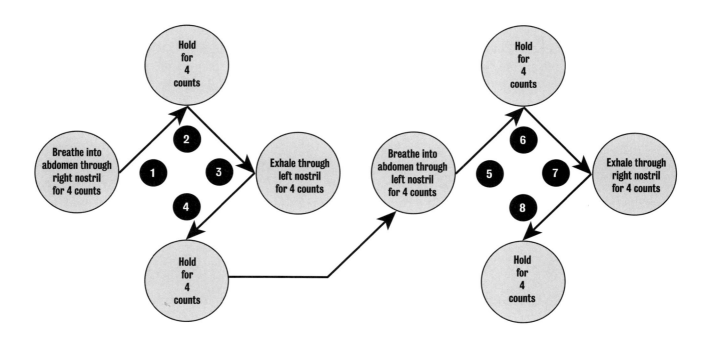

prior to listening to either CD, before any practice exam, at least once an hour during your actual exam, and whenever you need a relaxing and rejuvenating pick-me-up. Only do these stretches to the limits of your capabilities — if it hurts, don't stretch that far.

BAROQUE MUSIC

Numerous studies have shown that Baroque music, particularly selections in the 60Hz range, helps keep the mind in a state of relaxed concentration. This is the state of mind that facilitates learning and memorization. Throughout

Table 9 **YOGA STRETCHING EXAMPLES**

1. Mountain Pose	2. Rag Doll
• Sweep arms up over head • Feet shoulder width apart • Shoulder blades try to touch • Slightly tilt head back • Hold for 15 seconds	• Sweep your arms down and just hang near floor. (This is not a touch-your-toes stretch; it's just a hang.) • Hold for 15 seconds
3. Right Lunge	**4. Plank**
• Move hands forward on floor • Move right leg into lunge (stay on floor) • Left foot points forward and try to have your heel on the ground • Hold for 15 seconds	• Move your hands forward • Move the right leg back • Hold your body straight like a plank • Hold for 5 seconds
5. Cobra	**6. Left Lunge**
• Drop from plank onto floor • Put your hands under your shoulders and push your head and shoulders up • Arch your back and keep your hips on the floor • Hold for 15 seconds • Drop to the floor • Rise to knees, drop head on floor • Hold for 15 seconds	• Move up into a rag doll • Move left leg into lunge (stay on floor) • Right foot points forward and try to have heel on the ground • Hold for 15 seconds
7. Rag Doll	**8. Mountain Pose**
• Sweep your arms down and just hang near floor. (This is not a touch-your-toes stretch; it's just a hang.) • Hold for 15 seconds	• Sweep arms up over head • Feet shoulder width apart • Shoulder blades try to touch • Slightly tilt head back • Hold for 15 seconds

your study time, play quiet selections of Baroque classical music as background music. There are a number of CDs on the market that are designed specifically to enhance learning, and some have subliminal messages on them. Make sure you get CDs that are for focus and concentration.

PSYCHOACOUSTIC CDs

Brainwave patterns are an indicator of various states of consciousness. Using psychoacoustics, brainwaves can be trained so the user enters chosen states of consciousness. We create psychoacoustic audioprograms for our Accelerated PMP Exam Prep program using bilungual beats — that is, each ear hears different frequency beats. The middle brain hears the difference in the beats and this tunes the brain waves to the frequency of the desired brain state.

During the period of accelerated exam prep, you can stimulate two brainwave states to accelerate learning and improve retention. The first state you stimulate is called the alpha state, and the audio program we use to do that is called the Alpha Accelerator. In this state, you are in a relaxed, detached awareness and your mind is very receptive to new ideas and learning. The alpha state is the link between the subconscious and the conscious, so it provides a good medium to "reprogram" the subconscious. Many people have negative pre-conceptions regarding their test-taking abilities. When in an alpha state, you repeat in your mind a series of affirmations about your ability to stay calm and focused during your preparation and during your exam.

The second state you need to stimulate is called the delta state. Delta brainwaves exist during stages of deep, restorative sleep. A healthy mind needs to be in the delta state at least 40 minutes every day. You can also use the delta tapes to help you get very restful nights of sleep while you are in an accelerated exam prep program.

Both daytime and bedtime audio programs should be 30 minutes in length, and you should listen to both programs every day while you are studying.

You can create your own psychoacoustic audio programs at www.bwgen.com.

"Our delight in any particular study, art, or science rises and improves in proportion to the application which we bestow upon it. Thus, what was at first an exercise, becomes at length an entertainment."
— Joseph Addison

Structured Study Time

Visual Planning Techniques to Improve Test-Taking

We use techniques as outlined in Michelle LaBrosse's book, *Cheetah Project Management,* to enable people to plan their accelerated exam prep program. All the activities are performed at different times in various durations throughout your entire accelerated exam prep program and are brought into the test-taking environment to improve test-taking performance. The visual planning techniques presented below will enable you to quickly plan and implement your own accelerated exam preparation program. In order to create the plan, you incorporate much of what you have already done to achieve your peak performing mind, set up your rapid synthesis study aids, and incorporate relaxed focus techniques into your study program. We recommend you start and complete the plan at least a week before you start your accelerated exam prep immersion program.

STRUCTURED STUDY TIME PLAN OUTLINE

The plan includes:

- Determining the period of time you can set aside to completely immerse yourself in your study program.

- Identifying the space you can use for studying — this space must have a CD player, be comfortably heated or cooled, and be free from distractions.

- Planning your menu and purchasing food so that you can follow the diet guidelines to sustain a peak performing mind.

- Scheduling your complete 24-hour day for the duration of your accelerated exam prep program. Each day should include:
  - Meal/snack time
  - Exercise time
  - Content study time
  - Study techniques — mind maps, practice tests, Cheetah Sheet
  - Relaxation technique integration—breathing/yoga
  - Alpha Accelerator time
  - Delta Accelerator time

- Planning for exam day
  - Eat high protein breakfast
  - Get bottled water
  - Have Balance Bars and bring a nutritious high-protein lunch
  - Have sugar-free mints
  - Have paperwork to get into exam
  - Know where exam is

Record your plan on a wall poster for quick reference. This enables you to stay motivated and to focus on your exam prep activities. The figure shown below is a sample of a wall poster that you can use to record a shape-coded, color-coded, and size-coded accelerated exam prep plan.

ACTIVITY 6 — STRUCTURED STUDY PLAN

To develop your road map for studying, fill out the study plan tables on pages 33–35 first, modifying them as necessary to fit *your* daily schedule and then create a similar road map as shown in Figure 4 below.

Figure 4 **STRUCTURED STUDY PLAN ROADMAP**

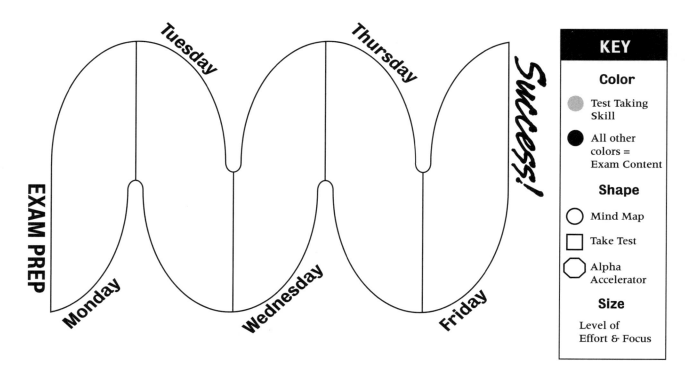

Table 10 **PRE-STUDY PREPARATIONS**

TASK 1.0 Pre-Study Preparations	DURATION	WHEN	YOUR DATE / TIME
1.1 Determine accelerated exam prep immersion time frame.	1 hour	A month before preparation, or however long you need to clear your calendar for the accelerated exam prep immersion.	
1.2 Identify and prepare your study space.	1 to 4 hours (depending on how messy it is)	A week or two before you start studying.	
1.3 Order reference materials and practice exams.	2 hours	2 to 3 weeks before you start studying (depends on shipping time).	
1.4 Peak performing mind preparations.	2 hours per week	Lifestyle changes — start a month before, shopping a day before.	
1.5 Mind map decisions (color-coding convention, timing).	4 hours	When you get the reference material, and at least 3 or 4 days before you start studying.	
1.6 Exam day planning. (You may have to schedule your exam, arrange for transportation and lodging near your exam, and find the exam location.)	4 to 10 hours	Do this far enough in advance so that you can get your exam scheduled when you want to take it — if you have a choice in the matter.	

Four — Structured Study Time

Table 11 **EXAMPLE DAILY STUDY SCHEDULE**

2.0 STUDY SCHEDULE — DAILY PLANNER		
Example of the level of detail you need to organize your study days during your accelerated prep immersion.		
Activity	**Duration**	**Time**
Exercise	60 minutes	0600-0700
Breakfast/shower	60 minutes	0700-0800
Practice exams	60 minutes	0800-0900
Relaxed focus excercise	10 minutes	0900-0910
Rapid synthesis / Content area 1	50 minutes	0910-1000
Snack/bio break	10 minutes	1000-1010
Relaxed focus excercise	10 minutes	1010-1020
Cheetah Sheet	20 minutes	1020-1040
Practice exams	60 minutes	1040-1140
Lunch	30 minutes	1140-1210
General reading, review, and general collaboration with others	30 minutes	1210-1240
Relaxed focus excercise	10 minutes	1240-1250
Rapid synthesis / Content area 2	50 minutes	1250-1340
Bio break/snack	10 minutes	1340-1350
Relaxed focused exercises	10 minutes	1350-1400
Daytime alpha accelerator audio program	35 minutes	1400-1435
Bio break/snack	10 minutes	1435-1445
Relaxed focus excercise	5 minutes	1445-1450
Cheetah Sheet	20 minutes	1450-1510
Practice exams	40 minutes	1510-1550
Bio break/snack/excercise	10 minutes	1550-1600
Rapid synthesis / Content area 3	50 minutes	1600-1650
Bio break/snack/excercise	10 minutes	1650-1700
Cheetah Sheet	10 minutes	1700-1710
Practice exams	40 minutes	1710-1750
Dinner	90 minutes	1750-1920
Evening walk	30 minutes	1920-1950
General reading, review. and collaboration with others	120 minutes	1950-2150
Bedtime delta audio program	30 minutes	2150-2220

Table 12 **YOUR DAILY STUDY SCHEDULE**

2.0 YOUR STUDY SCHEDULE — DAILY PLANNER		
Activity	Duration	Time

"I am always doing things I can't do, that's how I get to do them."
—Pablo Picasso

Conclusion & References

Getting Ready to Pass Your Test

You need a support team. If you live with others, you need to enroll them in your accelerated exam prep regimen. If they are supportive of your efforts, you will have much more success with your program. To get them on your side with this effort, share with them this workbook and let them help you plan your study time and your peak performing mind plan. If you share parenting, it is imperative you enroll your partner in your planning. It is your responsibility to develop contingency plans for child care during the time you have to focus on studying — very small children may not understand why you need time for quiet. You will fare far better if you have encouraging people around you while you pursue your goal of successfully passing your exam.

You can reduce your exam prep time and improve your exam performance for ANY exam, using the techniques outlined in this workbook.

- Focus on getting your mind in peak performing condition by paying attention to how your diet, exercise, and lifestyle impact your mental processing.

- Plan a structured study period setting up detailed time slots for studying.

- Include several rapid synthesis activities as an integral part of your exam prep.

- Set up your environment so you can maintain a state of alert, relaxed focus.

Use these techniques to develop a strong self-confidence for your exam performance that is grounded in following your comprehensive study program. Best of luck reaching your goals, FAST!!!!!

REFERENCES

- *Boost Your Brain Power*; Ellen Michaud, Russell Wild, and editors of Prevention Magazine; 1991, MJF Books.

- *Caffeine Blues*; Stephen Cherniske, M.S.; 1998, Warner Books.

- *Comedy Writing Secrets: How to Think Funny, Write Funny, Act Funny and Get Paid For It*; Melvin Helitzer; 1987, Writer's Digest Books.

- *The High Performance Mind*; Anna Wise; 1997, Tarcher/Putnam.

- *Limitless Learning: Making Powerful Learning an Everyday Event*; Doug McPhee; 1996, Zephyr Press.

- *Memory Pack: Everything You Need to Supercharge Your Memory and Master Your Life*; Andi Bell; 2000, Carlton Publishing Group.

- *Super Learning 2000*; Sheila Ostrander and Lynn Schroeder; 1994, Dell Books.

- *Total Recall: How to Maximize Your Memory Power*; Joan Minninger, Ph.D.; 1984, MJF Books.

Earn While You Learn

Now that you've experienced Cheetah's accelerated learning methodology for your exam prep, see how it can help you build the skills you need to excel at work. With Cheetah's online, instructor-led classes, you immediately apply what you learn to your own work projects.

Register at www.cheetahpm.com, and turn your potential into power at Cheetah speed.

Visit Our Web Site to Learn How to

Power Up Your Potential

Exam Preparation

Project Management Training

FREE Downloads

www.cheetahlearning.com